AMERICAN ORTHODOX

Finding the Ancient Faith in the Modern World

ROBERT JOHN HAMMOND

American Orthodox: Finding the Ancient Faith in the Modern World
Copyright © 2024 Robert Hammond

ISBN: 979-8-9919293-1-8

Published by:
New Way Press
http://www.NewWayPress.com
Sacramento, CA 95835

Cover photo by Sarah Stierch, Fort Ross State Historic Park Church, Jenner, California
Designed by Katherine Hyde

Printed in the United States of America

Acknowledgments

Special thanks to my wife, Lesa, who has read and reread all the drafts of this book and provided valuable suggestions, clarification, and feedback.

Many thanks to Simon Scionka and Silas Karbo, whose breathtaking documentary, *Sacred Alaska*, inspired me to write these stories about finding the ancient faith in the modern world. Thank you to Robin Innokentia and James Peter for sharing their stories with me. Thank you to Fr. Paul Volmensky, Fr. Timothy Winegar, and Fr. Ian MacKinnon for your suggestions and prayers. Thank you to Christine Gindi for her relentless support, encouragement, and assistance. Thanks also to Katherine Hyde for her professional editorial comments and assistance.

Above all, thanks to God and All Saints of North America for shining the Light and guiding the Way.

Contents

I am a Christian; I will not betray my faith.

—ST. PETER THE ALEUT

Introduction

In 2016, my life in the San Francisco Bay Area seemed to be on the brink of success. I had written books, worked on independent film projects, and taught screenwriting at the graduate level. Hollywood whispers promised grandeur—a Cecil B. DeMille biopic that could become a major feature film, even a television series. I signed the production contract, quit my teaching job, and waited for the spotlight to shine. But as quickly as those doors of opportunity had opened, they slammed shut. My dreams crumbled, leaving me debt-ridden, unemployed, and struggling with the haunting question: How did I wind up here?

Spiritually, emotionally, and financially, I was on the edge of a precipice. My once vibrant dreams turned to dust. In the silence, I prayed, pleading for direction and relief. The path ahead was shrouded in uncertainty, forcing me to rethink everything—my life, my beliefs, and my desires.

Unbeknownst to me, these dark times were the beginning of my journey to Orthodoxy. It started with a visit to a Greek festival, a YouTube video, and a simple internet search. A providential series of events led me to Holy Virgin Cathedral in San Francisco and then to an Orthodox baptism at Ascension Cathedral in Oakland. That baptism marked the first step on a long, winding spiritual path, one that would lead me through valleys of doubt and mountains of hope.

By 2024, I found myself in a small gathering at the home of my dear friend Robin Joy Innokentia Wellman, a historian at Fort Ross State Park. We were there for a private screening of the award-winning film *Sacred Alaska*, which had just won Best Feature Film at Byzanfest. As the film's images flickered on the screen and the haunting sounds of Orthodox hymns filled the room, I felt something stir deep within me.

In attendance were some of my closest friends: James, once a medicine man of the Chumash Tribe who had embraced Orthodox Christianity, and Kyle, a YouTuber known for his popular channel, *Orthocast*. Local Orthodox clergy mingled with parishioners, their voices mingling in hushed tones. This was more than a film viewing; it was a communion of souls, each of us united by a yearning to connect with the divine mysteries of Orthodoxy in the modern world.

As we shared food, fellowship, and stories of the saints who continue to inspire us, the idea for this book began to take shape. *Sacred Alaska* had ignited within me a flame that I could not extinguish. As a writer and filmmaker, I have always been drawn to narratives that plumb the depths of the human spirit, that illuminate the often-hidden intersections of faith and life. The lives of saints like Peter the Aleut, Innocent of Alaska, John of San Francisco, and Father Seraphim Rose resonated with my own spiritual journey—a quest for authenticity, for a faith that was as real and palpable as the air I breathed.

From my youth, superheroes and legends had always fascinated me. My imagination thrived on myth and fantasy, with comic books and Hollywood blockbusters providing an escape from the mundane. My academic pursuits only deepened this fascination, culminating in a screenplay about Cecil B. DeMille, the director who brought biblical epics to life. Yet, as life progressed, this fascination found new dimensions in Christ and the lives of the saints.

Christ, the Master of story, used parables that spoke directly to the heart, compelling His listeners to engage with the truths hidden within. As I moved closer to Orthodoxy, my love for the hero's journey found new life in the saints—real men and women who lived lives of extraordinary virtue and faith. In the Holy Virgin Cathedral in San Francisco, I knelt before the tomb of Saint John the Wonderworker, praying in a grand, holy space where the divine felt palpable. My prayers were answered in ways I could hardly have imagined, affirming the living presence of the saints.

The gathering at Robin's home was more than just an event; it was a moment of epiphany. I realized that the stories of the saints, the sacred sites scattered across California, and the journeys of those who had found solace in Orthodoxy were stories that needed to be told. This book is the fruit of that realization, a tapestry woven from the threads of faith, sacrifice, and miracles.

The Northern California coast, with its serrated cliffs and endless procession of waves, is a landscape rich with centuries of history. It's where Native American tribes flourished, Russian settlers established their outposts, and Orthodox Christianity found a foothold in the New World. Here, amidst the dramatic landscape, the lives of three individuals—a state historian, a former medicine man of the Chumash Tribe, and a struggling screenwriter—converge in a way that will change them forever. Their stories become intertwined with that of a little-known nineteenth-century saint, whose efforts to plant the seeds of Orthodox Christianity in America have left an indelible mark on its history and people.

In a world dominated by the relentless hum of Silicon Valley's technology and Hollywood's glittering facade, I discovered a faith unyielding to time's ceaseless march. The kaleidoscope of Orthodoxy stood as a sanctuary for souls seeking refuge from the ephemeral allure of contemporary existence. The vision of early missionaries like Saint Herman, Saint Innocent, and Saint Tikhon provides a roadmap for integrating Orthodoxy into the fabric of American life without losing its essence.

Orthodox Christianity's journey from the Great Commission to the present day is a saga of faith's resilience and adaptability. It began when Jesus Christ commanded His disciples to "go and make disciples of all nations," a mission that spread across the Roman Empire, flourished with Emperor Constantine's conversion, and reached the shores of California through Russian missionaries in 1812. Here, amidst the dramatic landscape, the seeds of Orthodox Christianity were planted, creating a spiritual legacy that endures to this day.

This book is not just a recounting of history; it is a narrative woven with the lives of people in the modern world who have collided with the ancient faith through the legacy of saints and sacred places. Together, we will walk through the sacred landscapes of Fort Ross, the bustling cities of California, and the remote monasteries that dot the American wilderness. Along the way, we will meet individuals whose lives have been profoundly shaped by the Orthodox faith, revealing how it continues to speak to the inmost longings of the human heart.

As you turn each page, may you find yourself drawn into the beauty, mystery, and depth of the Orthodox faith. This is not just a story of the past; it is a story being written every day in the lives of those who seek the ancient faith in the modern world. Welcome to the journey.

My Leap of Faith

It's later than you think. Harken, therefore, unto the work of God.

—FATHER SERAPHIM ROSE

Along the Central Coast of California near Santa Maria, the Pacific performs a symphony of grace. The waves rise and fall with a steady, melodic cadence, each one a note in a larger, divine composition. The ocean, expansive and vast, resonates with a tranquil beauty. The beaches, bathed in a soft, golden glow, stretch out like a holy altar, inviting all to pause and reflect on the quiet majesty of the sea.

The reverence of this setting mirrors the memory of my Protestant church baptism. "Do you believe that Jesus Christ was the only begotten Son of God, who died for your sins, was buried, and rose again on the third day?" The reverend's voice echoed off the cold tiles of the baptistery. The water was frigid, a shock to my eight-year-old body.

"Yes," I replied, my voice barely more than a whisper.

"I baptize you in the name of the Father, the Son, and the Holy Spirit."

The words disappeared as I sank beneath the surface, submerged in a world where the familiar melted away. The cold water surged into my nostrils, and I gagged, choking on the unexpected rush. I coughed, desperate for air, but the water held me under, as if it had a will of its own. The moments stretched into an eternity before I finally broke the surface, gasping for breath. In those brief seconds, I felt a disconnection, a sense of being overwhelmed by forces far greater than I could comprehend. I emerged from the water of life coughing and spitting, my face wet with tears and baptismal water. My sins had been washed away, or so I was told, but my young heart sensed something was missing.

My father, one of the first Black medical doctors in Santa Maria—a sleepy agricultural town named after the Holy Virgin Mary—had brought us to that church. The pastor welcomed us warmly, extending an invitation to join the congregation. Despite making friends with a few other Black families in town, we were a minority in both the church and my elementary school. The town, the church, and the people all felt foreign. I stood out in a sea of white faces, but I adapted quickly, making friends, excelling in school, and finding my place in this new world.

I attended Sunday school, memorized Bible verses, sang in the choir, and joined the Boy Scouts. I did all the things a good Christian boy was supposed to do. Yet as I grew older, a disquieting emptiness took hold of me. The simplicity of "believe in God and be good" felt hollow, a mere shadow of the

Christianity I read about in the New Testament. Where was the power? Where was the mystical experience? What did it truly mean to be baptized into a faith that demanded so much yet felt so little?

Rebellion was inevitable. I sought answers in every corner of the spiritual landscape. I dove headfirst into self-help programs, occult practices, Buddhism, Hinduism, and New Age spirituality. I meditated, chanted, practiced self-hypnosis, yoga, and Tai Chi. I devoured texts like the *Bhagavad Gita*, the *Tao Te Ching*, the *Lotus Sutra*, and *Autobiography of a Yogi*. Yet the more I sought, the more elusive the truth became.

I was adrift, unanchored, desperate for something solid, something real. After a year at Hampton University, a historically Black college in Virginia, and several stints in various jobs, cities, and relationships, I followed in my father's footsteps and joined the army. If I was going to die anyway, I reasoned, it might as well be in defense of something greater than myself— my country. America was in the throes of the Cold War, and I steeled myself to defend our nation against the threat of godless communism. But when I left the army, honorably discharged from Fort Carson, Colorado, I found myself in turmoil, both inwardly and outwardly.

One hot Fourth of July evening, I drove to Angel Stadium in Anaheim, California, to the Harvest Crusade, a sugar-coated millennial Christian rock concert led by superstar ex-surfer hippie Greg Laurie, pastor of one of Southern California's biggest megachurches. Harvest Fellowship was a spinoff from Chuck Smith's Calvary Chapel denomination, which grew out of the sixties Jesus People movement. Christian pop stars dominated the stage.

As the music reached a frenzied Christian rock crescendo, Greg Laurie culminated his emotional sermon about the wasted lives of glamorous pursuits and the value of sacrifice. The service ended with the impassioned altar call and hypnotic music urging everyone to repent and come down to the front so they could be prayed for and fill out cards with their contact information. I took comfort in the thought that I was already "saved" and didn't need to go back down to give my life to the Lord again. After all, once saved, always saved, I thought to myself as I headed back to the parking lot. Fireworks exploded over Angel Stadium, scintillating like jewels against the velvet night. Red, white, and blue explosions lit up the Fourth of July night sky above us, pop, pop, popping in the distance, fire in the heavens.

Without clear direction, my spiritual journey continued its erratic course through different denominations, philosophies, and practices. I was taught that true Christianity had vanished or been corrupted soon after the time of the Apostles, only to reappear during the Protestant Reformation. But as I looked further into the myriad interpretations and controversies that had sprung up over the centuries, I found myself caught in a maelstrom of doctrinal disputes, each one pulling me further away from the core of the faith.

My disillusionment with organized religion grew. I judged the moral and financial scandals that plagued the Vatican, the televangelists, and the megachurch pastors. I railed against the doomsday prophets who profited from end-times hysteria, their ever-changing dates for Christ's return ringing hollow. I was done with organized religion, even as I overlooked my own moral failings. Where was the true Christian church, the pillar and ground of truth?

Despite my waning confidence in religious institutions, I still believed in God and Christ. But how could I connect with the one supreme God amidst so many contradictory paths? My skepticism increased, skirting the edge of atheism, as despair threatened to consume me. I prayed for a sign, a glimpse of hope from on high. God, help me. Lord, have mercy.

On Memorial Day in 2016, my wife Lesa and I marked our anniversary by leaping out of a perfectly good airplane at 18,000 feet over Monterey Bay, California. Tumbling head over heels through the sky, I felt a silent stillness, a moment of pure surrender. Trusting in the parachute to bring me safely to earth required a leap of faith. Exhilaration gave way to triumph as I touched down on solid ground, heart pounding with the thrill of survival. I had no idea that the leap I was about to take in my spiritual life would make skydiving seem easy. Everything was about to change.

Was there a pillar and ground of truth beyond the chaos of manmade religions? In my search for early Christianity, I stumbled across a series of YouTube videos by Ted Nottingham, a former pastor of the First Christian Church who had converted to Orthodoxy. Ted's videos on Original Christianity pointed me toward the ancient traditions of the faith, the mystic monks of Mount Athos, and the Jesus Prayer. Could this be the truth I had been seeking all along? In all my searching, how had I missed this Eastern Orthodoxy?

I began my journey eastward, toward the Orthodox Church. I read Ted Nottingham's book *Written in our Heart: The Practice of Spiritual Transformation* and his translation of *The Prayer of the Heart: The Foundational Spiritual Mystery at the Core of Christianity* by Father Alphonse and Rachel Goettmann. I prayed the Jesus Prayer—"Lord Jesus Christ, Son of God, have mercy on me"—an ancient practice in Orthodox Christianity. I immersed myself in documentaries like *The Ancient Church*, talks by Metropolitan Kallistos Ware, and online sermons by Fr. Barnabas Powell, Metropolitan Jonah (Paffhausen), Abbot Tryphon, and Fr. Josiah Trenham. But I knew that to truly connect with this ancient faith, I needed more than books and videos. I needed a living community, fellowship in the fullness of the Church.

I opened my laptop, typed "Orthodox Christian churches near me" into Google, and hit enter. Boom! The screen filled with listings—Orthodox churches in every direction, in San Francisco, Berkeley, Concord, and Oakland. Where to begin? I was nervous. Some of these churches were ethnically based, with services conducted in languages I didn't understand. As a Black American who only spoke English, I wondered if I would find a place where I would feel welcome.

Then a memory surfaced—vivid, almost cinematic. Years before, soon after moving to the Bay Area, my wife and I had attended a Greek festival at what I thought was an Orthodox Church. The event had seemed like a fun cultural outing at the time. I recalled the lively atmosphere—the tantalizing aroma of souvlaki sizzling on the grill, the rhythmic beats of Greek music filling the air, the swirl of dancers in traditional costumes, their feet moving in perfect synchrony. The festival had been a feast for the senses, a celebration of life and culture, so different from anything I had experienced before.

But while the festival attendees reveled in the celebration, I had wandered off to explore the church itself. I remember standing in the center of the cathedral, gazing up at the icons that adorned the walls, their otherworldly gaze meeting mine. The scent of incense lingered in the air, a subtle reminder of something ancient, something sacred. But at the time, I was too caught up in my own spiritual pursuits, too convinced that I had already found the "truth." With a touch of arrogance, I had even left a little booklet in the church bookstore—*A Guide to True Peace: A Method of Attaining to Inward and Spiritual Prayer*—thinking that maybe someone there would discover the "truth" I believed I had found. Who was I to teach people with centuries of prayer and tradition how to pray? May God forgive me.

Irony dripped from that memory. Here I was, years later, standing at the crossroads of my spiritual journey, searching for the very truth I had once dismissed. Could it be that the answer had been right in front of me all along? Had I walked past it, blind to its presence, wrapped in the hubris of my own spiritual quest?

Little did I know at the time, but my path would once again cross that very church—Ascension Cathedral in Oakland, where I had once enjoyed the music, the baklava, and the dancing but had overlooked the spiritual treasures hidden within its walls.

I reached out to Fr. John Peck at the *Journey to Orthodoxy* blog for guidance. I also connected with Presbytera Judith Irene Matta at Descent of the Holy Spirit Orthodox Christian Mission in Santa Maria and Ted Nottingham at Inner Work for Spiritual Awakening. Fr. John Peck referred me to Fr. Michael Anderson at Saint Christina of Tyre Orthodox Church in Fremont, California. He recommended the books *Light from the Christian East* by James Peyton and *Orthodox Spirituality* by Metropolitan Hierotheos. Despite the forty-mile drive from Walnut Creek, I met with Fr. Michael, who welcomed me into the church, offering insights and referring me to other Orthodox communities in the area. He encouraged me to read the Didache, an early Christian text, and to listen to podcasts on Ancient Faith Radio, especially those by the late Fr. Thomas Hopko. He also suggested watching the Russian film *Ostrov* (*The Island*), a moving story about a man tortured with shame who finds redemption in a remote island monastery.

As I left my meeting with Fr. Michael, my phone rang. It was Fr. Marin from Saint Demetrios Greek Orthodox Church in Concord. We scheduled a meeting for the following week. When I entered the church, I was overwhelmed by the sight of the Christ Pantocrator icon on the domed ceiling. I wept in awe and repentance, tears flowing freely as Father Marin led me through the Lord's Prayer. He put his arm around me and welcomed me home, encouraging me to continue my journey with faith and humility. He recommended the documentary *Mysteries of the Jesus Prayer* by Norris Chumley and *Introduction to Orthodoxy* videos by Frederica Mathewes-Green. I also visited the Holy Virgin Cathedral in San Francisco, where I venerated the relics of Saint John of San Francisco. At the cathedral's bookstore, I purchased my first icons and prayer rope.

Ted Nottingham connected me with Fr. Philip Tolbert in Santa Rosa, who in turn referred me to Fr. Tom Zaferes at Ascension Cathedral in Oakland. Fr. Tom invited me to attend Divine Liturgy the following Sunday, which just happened to be the Feast of St. John the Theologian, my patron saint. The service was breathtaking, a sensory immersion into the heavenly realms. Though the congregation was primarily of Greek descent, it was diverse enough for me to feel at ease. Everyone spoke English, and I was warmly greeted by several parishioners. I continued attending services at Ascension Cathedral, meeting with Fathers Tom Zaferes and Ninos Oshana for biweekly Orthodox Faith classes and Bible studies. It was there that I met my godfather, Athan Magannas.

As I continued my journey into Orthodoxy, I reflected on that Greek festival I had attended years earlier. I turned to Lesa and asked, "Wasn't that an Orthodox church where we went to the Greek festival?" She nodded. "Yes, that was at the church you're attending now." I was stunned.

Even though I had read the Bible cover to cover multiple times and attended countless studies as a Protestant, I began to understand that Orthodox Christianity was something entirely different. It wasn't just a legal system offering a "get out of jail free" card from an angry judge. The Church was more like a hospital, healing the sick and brokenhearted, always welcoming the prodigal back into the loving arms of the Father. With prayer and fasting, I prepared for baptism into the Orthodox Church. I devoured spiritual texts like *The Way of a Pilgrim,* the Desert Fathers, and an abridged version of *The Philokalia*. Throughout the day, I prayed the Jesus Prayer: "Lord Jesus Christ, have mercy on me." I was on my way home.

The week leading up to my baptism was spent in prayer and fasting, immersing myself in self-reflection, repentance, and humility. On the night before my baptism, Lesa and I attended the Ascension Cathedral Christmas concert, which lifted my spirits and set the tone for my reception into the Church. I made a life confession with Fr. Tom just before the baptism, unburdening myself of every sin I could recall. The exorcism stage at the entrance of the church was an emotional experience, waves of repentance and tears washing over me as I renewed my commitment to Christ. I affirmed the Nicene-Constantinopolitan Creed, declaring my faith in One God, the Father Almighty, and in Jesus Christ, His only begotten Son.

On Saturday, December 3, 2016, I was received into the Orthodox Church through Holy Baptism, taking on the name of my patron saint, John the Theologian. The next morning, I received my first communion, approaching the Holy Chalice with lighted candles in the company of my godfather, Athan. The experience left me with a sense of homecoming, resting in God's grace.

I was blissful and content with my new home at Ascension Cathedral, our condo in Walnut Creek, and my career as a writer and part-time professor. I was ready to settle into a semi-retired, comfortable life. But just as quickly as I found stability, it was shaken once again. Several major projects fell through, our income plummeted, and I needed to find full-time work.

I prayed to St. John the Wonderworker of San Francisco for guidance.

Four days after my baptism, I attended a job interview in Sacramento, the city named after the Blessed Sacrament. A few weeks later, I accepted a position helping veterans and their families connect with benefits and resources. I loved the job, but the seventy-mile daily commute each way was unsustainable. So we started looking for a place to live closer to work. Using my veteran's benefits, we were able to buy a home in Sacramento and move in thirty days with no money down.

Settling into our new city, I searched for a new Orthodox parish. A quick Google search for "Orthodox Church near me" revealed a multitude of options. Holy Ascension Russian Orthodox Church was just a few blocks from my new job, and Elevation of the Holy Cross was a ten-minute drive from our new house.

As I walked by Holy Ascension one day, I noticed Fr. Paul Volmensky in the yard. I introduced myself, mentioning that I was new to Sacramento and had just started working nearby. He warmly invited me inside the church and encouraged me to attend the upcoming Sunday Liturgy, which happened to fall on the Feast of St. John the Theologian, my patron saint. The following week, I visited Elevation of the Holy Cross, where I met Archpriest Fr. Ian MacKinnon, who had founded the first Orthodox church in my hometown of Santa Maria. After Fr. Ian retired, Fr. Timothy Winegar was ordained as the parish priest. Years later, I brought my mother and sister to visit Orthodox Church of the Annunciation, where Fr. Ian had first introduced our community to the ancient faith.

In 2021, I witnessed as my first two godchildren, Mark and Aquilla (Xenia), were baptized at Elevation of the Holy Cross. Both had been adult converts from Protestantism, their journeys reflecting my own search for truth.

As I continued to grow in my faith, I realized that this journey was not just about my own salvation. It was about sharing the light of Orthodoxy with others, bringing them along on this path toward the fullness of faith.

What Is a Saint According to the Orthodox Church?

For God is not the author of confusion, but of peace, as in all churches of the saints.

(1 CORINTHIANS 14:33)

When I was a Protestant Christian, sainthood seemed a distant concept, reserved for historical figures and martyrs of old, their lives shrouded in the mists of antiquity. Saints were echoes of faith, their relevance confined to the pages of history. My journey into Orthodoxy, however, unveiled a vibrant tapestry of holy men and women whose lives were not just historical artifacts but living testaments to a faith that was present and active in the world. This revelation was not merely academic; it was transformative, reshaping the contours of my spiritual journey.

My first encounter with this living tradition occurred at Holy Virgin Cathedral in San Francisco. As I crossed the threshold, the scent of incense greeted me, mingling with the warm glow of candlelight. The sanctuary was alive with reverence, the air thick with the presence of the divine. It was here that I began to understand what it meant to be a saint in the Orthodox Church.

A kind parishioner guided me to the relics of St. John the Wonderworker, a Russian bishop whose life and miracles had left an indelible mark on those who knew him. As I stood before his relics, it seemed as though the veil between heaven and earth had been momentarily lifted. In that sacred space, the concept of sainthood took on a new, dynamic meaning for me. Saints were not distant or inaccessible—they were near, their presence palpable and real.

My prayers to St. John were answered in ways that defied my expectations. Within months, I found myself with a new job and a home in Sacramento, blessings I attributed to his intercession. This personal experience was a powerful affirmation of the Orthodox belief in the ongoing presence and assistance of the saints.

In Orthodox theology, sainthood is not about infallibility but about reflecting the love of Christ. Saints are those who have allowed God's grace to work through their imperfections, becoming beacons of faith and compassion. Their lives are testimonies to the transformative power of divine love, and their intercessions are sought not out of superstition but out of a sense of spiritual kinship.

The Church does not create saints; it recognizes those whom God has glorified. From the righteous ancestors of Christ to modern-day ascetics, the saints encompass a wide spectrum of human experience. They include prophets, apostles, martyrs, bishops, priests, and laypeople, all united by their unwavering love for God and their neighbors.

My journey from Protestantism to Orthodoxy was marked by a discovery of the saints, whose lives and intercessions became a guiding light. Through venerating their relics and embracing the tradition of a patron saint, I found a supernatural connection to the divine and a new sense of purpose.

The saints of the Orthodox Church are not distant, ethereal beings but living witnesses to the transformative power of Christ's love. They inspire us to strive for holiness, to seek God's grace in our everyday lives, and to remember that we are all called to be saints, reflecting the light of Christ in a world in desperate need of hope and redemption.

Saint Peter the Aleut

The blood of the martyrs is the seed of the Church.

—TERTULLIAN, AD 197

The story of St. Peter the Aleut begins in the vast land-scapes of Alaska, where the Orthodox faith took root through the efforts of missionaries such as St. Herman. Born into the Kodiak community, Peter—originally named Chuk-agnak—was baptized into the Orthodox Christian faith at a young age. His life, though brief, would stand as a powerful tes-tament to unwavering faith and the ultimate sacrifice.

Under the spiritual guidance of St. Herman, who had estab-lished a monastic community on Kodiak, Peter grew in both strength and devotion. The monks lived simply, dedicated to prayer, labor, and nurturing the spiritual lives of the Native people. Among their spiritual children, Peter stood out, his strong character and firm faith marking him as someone with the potential for great spiritual resolve.

Life in Kodiak was a constant interplay between beauty and hardship, where the rhythms of the sea dictated the lives of the native Alaskan people, who were skilled hunters and fishermen. Peter, like many young men his age, embraced the challenges of the sea, his faith ever-present in his heart. The small village church, filled with the scent of incense and adorned with icons, became a sanctuary where the saints were not mere images but living presences guiding his life.

In 1812, the Russian-American Company established Fort Ross in California, an outpost created to exploit the rich waters for sea-otter furs, provide food for Russian Alaska through farming and ranching, and establish trade with Spanish missions as well as American and English ships. This outpost, located about 50 miles north of San Francisco, was the southernmost extension of Russian America. The Spanish colonists, wary of Russian encroachment, viewed this presence with suspicion and saw it as a potential threat to their control over the region.

By 1815, Peter, now an experienced hunter despite his youth, joined a group of Aleut hunters on an expedition far from home, traveling to the southern coast of California, deep within Spanish-controlled territory. The Spanish missionaries, zealous in their efforts to convert indigenous peoples to Catholicism, viewed these Orthodox Christian hunters with suspicion.

Peter was among about fifteen hunters who, after a disappointing otter hunt in the Channel Islands, decided to venture to the mainland near Los Angeles, despite warnings about hostile Spaniards. The group was soon captured by Spanish soldiers, and Peter received a severe head wound during the confrontation. Faced with the ultimatum to convert to Catholicism or face torture, all but Peter and one companion chose to convert. The local Chumash Indians were forced to carry out the gruesome torture, cutting off Peter's fingers and toes, joint by joint. Throughout his agony, Peter remained resolute, declaring, "I am a Christian. I will not deny my faith!" Eventually, they disemboweled him.

Peter's steadfast refusal to abandon his faith, even under the most excruciating torture, left a profound impact on those who survived, particularly his Kodiak compatriot, Ivan Kyglaia. Kyglaia would later recount Peter's courage and resolute faith, which served as a beacon of inspiration for the Orthodox Christian community. The story of St. Peter the Aleut, a tale of ultimate sacrifice, echoes through the ages, reminding the faithful of the power of unwavering belief in the face of unimaginable suffering.

Ivan Kyglaia sat silently as he recounted the horror that had unfolded before his eyes. His voice trembled with the memory, the images of that brutal day seared into his mind forever. "They cut off his fingers, his hands . . . and then they opened his stomach," he whispered, the pain of recollection evident in every word.

He had watched, helpless, as the Spanish soldiers inflicted unspeakable pain on his friend, Chukagnak. And yet, through it all, Peter had not uttered a word of renunciation. Even as they cut into his flesh, even as they tortured him, his lips moved in silent prayer.

Kyglaia had expected the same fate. But at the moment when he thought his end had come, a priest arrived, bearing a note. The priest read the paper and then ordered that it be buried with Peter's body. The soldiers obeyed, and for reasons unknown to Kyglaia, he was spared.

After Peter's death, Kyglaia was taken back to the mission, where he was held in a filthy jail cell. Days passed in a blur of hunger and despair. When he was finally moved to Santa Barbara, he found no trace of his Kodiak comrades. They had been transferred to Monterey, leaving him alone in the hands of his captors.

But Kyglaia was determined not to meet the same fate as Peter. Together with another Kodiak, Philip Atash'sha, he devised a plan to escape. The two men managed to steal a baidarka, a small skin-covered kayak, and paddled south to San Pedro, where they had originally been captured. From there, they continued to Catalina Island, then on to Santa Barbara Island, and finally to San Nicolas Island.

The journey was grueling, the open sea merciless, but the men's determination carried them forward. The weather was favorable, and the native people of San Nicolas Island welcomed their arrival. For a time, they lived among the islanders, hunting cormorants and using their meat for food and their skins for clothing. Yet the ordeal had taken its toll. Atash'sha died after a year on the island, leaving Kyglaia alone once more.

In the fall of 1818, two Spanish ships anchored off San Nicolas Island. The ships' crews came ashore in rowboats, but Kyglaia, with the help of the islanders, managed to stay hidden. He watched as the Spanish gathered plants that grew in the grass, seemingly oblivious to his presence. Later, another ship arrived, its crew offering Kyglaia passage. But he was afraid—no one on board spoke Russian or any of the Kodiak languages, and he feared that the offer might be a trap.

Finally, in May 1819, the brig *Il'mena* arrived, sent by the Russian-American Company to retrieve hunting crews. Kyglaia was rescued at last, and he returned to Fort Ross, where he gave a full deposition of the events leading up to Peter's martyrdom. His testimony, provided with the help of interpreters Ivan Samoilov and Iakov Shelechov, would later become the basis for Peter's glorification as a saint.

After his rescue, Kyglaia made his way back to Alaska, his journey long and perilous, each step a battle against the elements and the haunting memories of what had transpired. When he finally reached Spruce Island, he recounted the harrowing tale to St. Herman. The elder monk listened in silence, his face a mask of sorrow and reverence. When the story was finished, St. Herman stood before the icon of Christ, tears filling his eyes. He made the sign of the cross and said solemnly, "Holy New Martyr Peter, pray to God for us!"

News of Peter's martyrdom spread quickly through the Orthodox community, reaching even the farthest corners of Alaska. His story became a symbol of steadfast faith and divine grace, inspiring countless believers. The memory of his sacrifice was honored in prayers and hymns, his name spoken with reverence and awe.

The life of St. Peter the Aleut is celebrated in hymns that capture the essence of his faith and sacrifice. One such hymn praises his steadfastness, his unyielding devotion to Christ, even in the face of unimaginable suffering. His story, passed down through generations, continues to inspire and guide those who seek a greater understanding of faith and devotion.

In 1980, the Orthodox Church glorified Peter as a saint, recognizing his martyrdom and his unshakable faith. He became the first Native American martyr of North America, a beacon of faith whose light would shine through the ages.

The deposition of Ivan Kyglaia, recorded at Fort Ross, remains the sole eyewitness account of Peter's martyrdom. It is a document of pain, loss, and ultimate triumph—a testimony to the strength of faith in the face of brutal persecution. And as the years passed, the memory of Peter the Aleut grew, not only in the hearts of the Orthodox faithful but in the annals of history, where his sacrifice would never be forgotten.

The Fire and the Sea

It is he that buildeth his stories in the heaven,
and hath founded his troop in the earth;
he that calleth for the waters of the sea,
and poureth them out upon the face of the earth:
The Lord is his name.

(AMOS 9:6)

The small room at Holy Assumption Monastery in Calistoga, California, was dimly lit by flickering candles, casting a warm, serene glow over the faces of those gathered. The scent of incense lingered in the air, creating an atmosphere of reverence. Among the group, an artist named Chris began to recount his story, his voice steady but laden with the weight of what he was about to share.

Chris, a man of Kodiak descent, was rooted in his heritage and traditions. His hands, calloused from years of work and creation, had shaped many pieces of art that connected the present with the past, embodying the spirit of his ancestors.

His girlfriend, a woman of the Chumash Tribe, sat beside him, her presence a silent support as he delved into the tale that had brought him to this moment.

For years, Chris had been haunted by the story of St. Peter the Aleut, a tale passed down through generations—a story of faith, sacrifice, and martyrdom. It was a narrative that intertwined with his Native heritage, creating a tapestry of reverence and sorrow. The martyrdom of St. Peter, a symbol of unwavering faith in the face of brutal torture and death, ignited a fire within Chris that he could not extinguish.

In the summer of 2016, Chris was invited to exhibit his work at a prestigious art show in Berkeley, California. The theme was extremely personal: the intersection of indigenous identity and spirituality. For this, he chose to depict the martyrdom of St. Peter the Aleut, not only through paint but through wood, the living material that had been a part of his life since childhood. With every stroke of his chisel, he felt the weight of history bearing down on him, the cries of his ancestors mingling with the chants of monks, the scent of incense blending with the salt air of Kodiak.

The finished icon was breathtaking—a depiction of St. Peter in the triumph of his transcendent life, his face a portrait of serene defiance, holding a cross to show his martyrdom. His hand was raised to show that it was fully restored in the resurrection. Chris had engraved the icon into a large wooden board, smooth from years of being caressed by the Pacific waves, now bearing the indelible marks of his creation. The icon was not just a work of art; it was a bridge between past and present, a testament to both reconciliation and remembrance.

Saint Peter the Aleut

The art show in Berkeley was a success, attracting admirers from all walks of life. Yet for Chris, the icon was never meant to remain in the hands of others. It was a creation born of his soul and tradition—a tradition that demanded he return it to the earth, to release it back to nature from whence it came.

When the show ended, Chris knew what he had to do. With his girlfriend by his side, he drove from Berkeley to the northern coast of California, to the jagged cliffs near Fort Ross. The journey was long, marked by silence and the rhythmic pounding of their hearts. The coastal fog curled around their car as they wound their way through the ancient redwoods, the trees standing like sentinels watching over their pilgrimage.

Upon reaching the beach, Chris was greeted by the roar of the Pacific, the waves crashing against the rocks with a force that echoed in his bones. He gathered driftwood, carefully constructed a pyre, and set it ablaze. The flames leaped into the air, fierce and hungry, as if eager to consume the offering he was about to place upon them.

But as Chris laid the icon atop the fire, a strange thing happened. The flames danced around it, teasing the wood, but the icon would not burn. The fire, which had eagerly devoured the driftwood, recoiled from the icon, leaving it untouched, unscathed. Chris stared in disbelief, the crackling of the flames filling his ears, the heat pressing against his skin, but the icon remained as it was—a symbol of something greater, something beyond his understanding.

"Everything else burned," he whispered, the group now silent, every listener enraptured. "The wood, the kindling, all of it. But not the icon. It was a miracle."

Chris's heart raced as he watched the flames refuse their prize. He could see the face of St. Peter the Aleut staring back at him, serene and resolute, just as he had carved it. But this was not how it was supposed to end. The tradition demanded the release, the return to nature. Desperation gnawed at him as he realized what he must do.

Turning to the ocean, Chris hefted the icon in his hands, feeling its weight, both physical and spiritual. His girlfriend stood by, understanding the gravity of the moment. He walked to the edge of the shore, where the waves surged and retreated, a never-ending cycle of life and death. With a cry that was torn from the depths of his soul, he hurled the icon into the sea, watching as it splashed down, caught in the surf, and was slowly pulled away by the currents.

The ocean accepted the offering with the same quiet indifference it had shown to countless others over the millennia. Chris stood there, his breath coming in ragged gasps, his eyes fixed on the spot where the icon had disappeared beneath the waves. The fire behind him crackled and hissed, but the roar of the Pacific drowned it out, leaving only the sound of the ocean and the wind as his companions.

In that moment, Chris felt a wave of peace wash over him, mingled with sorrow. He had fulfilled his tradition, releasing the icon back to the elements, but he knew that its memory would remain with him forever. The image of St. Peter the Aleut, carved into the wood with such love and pain, drifted somewhere beneath the waves, perhaps to be carried across the seas, perhaps to sink into the depths, but always to remain a part of the earth and the ocean from which it had come.

As Chris turned away from the shore, his girlfriend joined him, slipping her hand into his. Her eyes, filled with understanding, met his, and in that gaze, he saw the connection of their shared histories—a bond forged in fire and sealed by the sea.

Together, they walked back to the fire, now dying down to embers, the last vestiges of its fury spent. The ocean continued to crash against the shore, a ceaseless reminder of the world beyond, of the stories untold and the spirits that lingered. But for Chris, there was only silence and the knowledge that he had done what he was meant to do.

And as they made their way back to their car, the icon of St. Peter the Aleut was carried away by the waves, seemingly lost to the sea, yet forever etched into the heart of the artist who had dared to carve it.

A Journey Home

Listen to me, O coastlands, pay attention, you peoples from far away! The LORD called me before I was born, while I was in my mother's womb he named me.

(ISAIAH 49:1)

The air buzzed with anticipation at the Elevation of the Holy Cross Orthodox Church in Sacramento on December 13, 2018, the Feast of St. Herman. The scent of incense wove through the church like an ancient spirit, mingling with the solemn yet joyous hymns that echoed against the wooden beams, wrapping the congregation in a sacred embrace. It was within this mystical atmosphere that I first saw James.

He stood out, not just for his composed demeanor but for the quiet intensity in his eyes—a reflection of a soul deeply searching. A young Native American, James's journey had been long and winding, leading him through various spiritual paths, and now, for the first time, into an Orthodox church.

As he crossed the threshold, I felt an instinctive pull to approach him. "Welcome," I said, extending my hand. "I'm John."

His eyes met mine with a contemplative light. "James," he replied, his voice steady and thoughtful.

I showed him how to make the Orthodox sign of the cross—three fingers representing the Holy Trinity, moving from forehead to midsection and from right shoulder to left. After the Liturgy, I introduced him to Fr. Timothy Winegar. James's story flowed easily—his days as a Native American medicine man, his explorations of Roman Catholicism and Protestantism, and now his tentative steps into Orthodoxy, a path as ancient as his own heritage.

James had grown up immersed in the traditions of his people, the Chumash and Gabrielino-Tongva tribes. From an early age, he was taught to cleave to the Truth—a foundational principle of his ancestors' ancient religion. As he matured, he recognized that many elders had seamlessly integrated Christianity into their cultural practices. This realization sparked in him a desire to pursue Christianity, leading to his baptism in the Catholic Church.

Yet, despite his commitment to the Christian life, James felt something was missing. Over time, his path led him to discover the Orthodox Church. When he first entered the Elevation of the Holy Cross in Sacramento, an icon of All Saints of North America caught his eye. Among the saints depicted was St. Peter the Aleut, whose image seemed to reach out to him, evoking a sense of familiarity and connection. This was no coincidence; it was a signpost on his spiritual journey.

At that time, an icon of St. Peter, recently discovered by Fort Ross historian Robin Joy Wellman, was temporarily at Holy Ascension Church in Sacramento. I frequently encouraged James to go and venerate the icon. Finally, on the very last day before the icon was to be returned to the Holy Assumption Monastery in Calistoga, James decided to visit. When Robin stood up to explain the connection between St. Peter and the Channel Islands, as well as Los Angeles, James knew he had to speak with her. This was the homeland of his ancestors. That moment marked the beginning of a long and transformative friendship. As their conversations continued, St. Peter's presence in James's life became undeniable. It was clear that St. Peter was guiding him toward a greater understanding of his faith.

James's journey toward Orthodoxy was more than a quest for spiritual truth; it was a homecoming. The faith he had sought so fervently was now revealing itself in the ancient practices and teachings of the Orthodox Church, resonating with the traditions of his ancestors. The pieces of his spiritual puzzle began to fall into place, each one guided by the hand of St. Peter the Aleut.

On St. Herman's Day, December 13, 2019, James was baptized at Elevation of the Holy Cross Church by Father Timothy Winegar and Abbot Damascene of St. Herman of Alaska Monastery. The moment was one of overwhelming transformation. He took the name Peter, acknowledging the saint who had become a guiding light on his journey. Robin and I were there to witness this sacred moment, feeling the weight of history and faith converge as James immersed himself in the waters of baptism.

As Peter embraced the Orthodox faith, he found a sense of peace and fulfillment that had eluded him for so long. The former medicine man had found the medicine for his soul. Even though he was one of the few, if not the only, Chumash Tribe members that he knew of in the Orthodox Church, his story, woven with history and personal transformation, became a testament to the enduring power of faith and the profound connections that span cultures and centuries.

Inspired by Peter's journey, his younger sister also embraced Orthodoxy. She was baptized Olga, after St. Olga of Alaska, in 2024 at St. Timothy's Antiochian Church in Lompoc, California, by Fr. John Valadez. This marked a significant moment in their family's spiritual journey, symbolizing a return to an ancient faith that resonated deeply with their Native American heritage.

On April 9, 2024, Peter traveled with Abbot Damascene to St. Herman of Alaska Monastery in Platina, California, to explore monastic life. Immersed in the rhythms of monastic prayer and work, Peter found a peace that had eluded him for much of his life. The monastery, founded by Fr. Seraphim Rose, nestled in the mystic mountains of Northern California, became his sanctuary. Here, Peter delved deeper into his faith, embracing the ancient monastic traditions that had sustained countless souls before him.

Peter's journey had brought him full circle. He returned to the spiritual traditions of his ancestors, embraced the Christian faith that had shaped much of his life, and finally discovered the deep well of Orthodoxy. Here, he found the spiritual medicine he had sought for so long. His story is one not just of conversion but of transformation—finding a home for his soul in a faith that bridges the past and the present, the sacred and the everyday.

Robin Innokentia Wellman at Fort Ross with an icon of St. Peter the Aleut

The Water of Repentance

ROBIN BECOMES INNOKENTIA

Ye have not chosen me, but I have chosen you, and ordained you, that ye should go and bring forth fruit, and that your fruit should remain: that whatsoever ye shall ask of the Father in my name, he may give it you.

(JOHN 15:16)

September 9, 2016—Fort Ross, California

The surf collided violently with the battered rocks, each impact resonating along the cliffs of Fort Ross, California, echoing the turmoil within Robin's heart. A fair-skinned woman of Irish descent with reddish-brown hair that danced in the salty breeze, Robin's eyes mirrored the sadness that weighed on her soul. Each step along the beach was heavy with the memories of a life soon to be left behind.

As she was about to leave the beach, she had an urge to turn around and face the ocean again, and something caught her

49

eye—a glint of light reflecting off the distant sand. Distracted and annoyed that someone might have discarded trash on this sacred beach, Robin quickened her pace. The mysterious object, half-buried and gleaming, beckoned her closer. Robin's emotions overwhelmed her, and she fell to her knees. Tears streaming down her cheeks, she brushed away the grains of sand to reveal the wooden image of St. Peter the Aleut. The intricately painted face of the saint looked back at her, serene and steadfast.

She clutched the icon to her chest, her sobs harmonizing with the crashing waves. She kissed the wooden surface tenderly, gazing longingly out to the expansive, indifferent sea. Each teardrop that fell mingled with the sand as the waves continued their timeless assault on the rocks. Robin knew St. Peter's story very well. She had told it many times. As she turned to look out at the ocean her mind's eye brought it into view . . .

1812—Bodega Bay, California

The scene shifted back in time, to a coastline similar yet different. The ocean swelled and broke with force against the golden shoreline, its rhythmic assault echoing through the coastal air, heralding the arrival of a sailing ship in the distance. The vessel flew the white, blue, and red flag of the Russian-American Company, its double-eagle symbol proud against the sky.

The ship's crew—Russian sailors, crewmen, and Native Alaskan workers—disembarked, carrying supplies ashore. Among them was Saint Peter the Aleut, then known as Chukagnak, a cross hanging from his neck. As his feet touched the land, St. Peter bowed low and made the sign of the cross, his prayer merging with the sound of the waves.

2016—Fort Ross

Robin slowly stood, holding the icon in front of her. The sound of waves crashing against the rocky coast of Fort Ross echoed in her ears, just as it had for St. Peter the Aleut, creating a timeless melody that underscored her journey. Robin's life was intimately connected to the history and spiritual legacy of Fort Ross, reflecting the enduring presence of Orthodoxy in America. For over thirty years, she had dedicated herself to teaching about the diverse tribal peoples of the Northwestern Pacific, the Native people in Alaska, and the significant Russian influence in California.

Robin was born in Fresno and raised in Sacramento, a California girl through and through. Her upbringing was rooted in Christianity, with both grandparents serving as ministers in the Pentecostal Assembly of God. Her grandmother, a trailblazer, was among the first women to attend seminary and become a minister. Her closeknit family was emotional and affectionate, prone to lots of hugs and kisses. These early experiences instilled in Robin a strong, Jesus-centered faith that would shape her entire life.

At nineteen, Robin moved to the coast, married, and embraced a rustic lifestyle. This move eventually brought her to Fort Ross in 1990, not because of a passion for history, but due to a promising opportunity with the California State Parks Department. Initially, she had little interest in the fort's history, but her love for nature, working with children, and learning

about Native American culture kept her engaged. As she set-
tled into her role, however, she became increasingly captivated
by the stories and legacy of Fort Ross, especially its ties to the
Orthodox Christian faith.

Robin's introduction to Orthodoxy came through her work
as a historian, which required her to delve into the history of
the land and its diverse peoples. As she learned more, her interest in the Orthodox Church grew. In 1990, during a visit from
Archbishop Anthony of San Francisco, she made an innocent
mistake that would spark a lasting relationship with the Orthodox clergy. As a naturally affectionate person, she greeted the
archbishop with bread and salt in the traditional way but then
followed up with a hug—unaware that Orthodox bishops are
traditionally greeted with a bow and a kiss on the hand. The
archbishop's initial surprise quickly turned into warmth, as
he forgave the breach of protocol with humility and kindness.
From that day on, he fondly referred to Robin as "that young
girl" whenever he visited.

Over the years, Robin's interactions with the Orthodox
clergy who frequented Fort Ross for liturgies and pilgrimages
were always marked by mutual respect and kindness. Despite
not being Orthodox herself, she felt a sense of belonging among
the priests and parishioners. Her responsibilities at Fort Ross
expanded to include cleaning the church, organizing presen-
tations, and even firing the fort's cannon for visiting clergy—a
tradition that brought joy to all involved.

Robin's connection to Orthodoxy developed naturally. The
clergy never pressured her to convert from her Protestant
faith; instead, they welcomed her with open arms, patiently

answering her questions and inviting her into their community. Their gentle, loving approach allowed Robin to explore her faith at her own pace. As a historian, she traveled to Russia more than a dozen times, meeting with priests, bishops, historians, and museum directors. She led countless academic groups and several Orthodox pilgrimages of clergy and monastics to Russia and various parts of Eastern Europe. Despite her immersion in Orthodox culture and her longstanding relationships with clergy and monastics in the US and beyond, Robin never considered converting to Orthodoxy.

For decades, Robin served the Fort Ross community with a sincere love for the land, its history, and the thousands of pilgrims who visited each year. On the fateful day when she discovered the icon of St. Peter in the sand, she was tearfully saying goodbye to the place she had loved and lived in for thirty years.

In 2016, Robin was told that her position with the California State Parks Department would be ending, which meant that her thirty-year career at Fort Ross would end. She sat, stunned and silent, holding back tears as her supervisor told her the job was being eliminated due to budget cuts and reorganization. As her time at Fort Ross neared its end, Robin experienced a sense of grief and sadness, mixed with a moment of connection with the divine. That was when, while walking along the beach, she spotted something glinting in the sand. Crossing a storm-swollen creek in her rain boots, she discovered the half-buried icon of St. Peter the Aleut washed ashore.

After much prayer, Robin decided that the best home for the icon would be Holy Assumption Monastery in Calistoga, California, whose chapel is modeled on the Fort Ross Chapel. With

Archbishop Benjamin of San Francisco's blessing, the nuns of the monastery agreed. The icon became a symbol of comfort and faith. After numerous false claims, Robins eventually heard from the artist who painted the icon and he told the story to her and the nuns at the Monastery. The icon's miraculous appearance on the beach and the story behind it—the failed attempt by the artist to burn the icon as part of a traditional ceremony—underscored the mystical connections that had always surrounded her.

"Two different priests told me," Robin said, "that I did not find the icon. St. Peter found me."

The gathered listeners shivered, feeling the weight of those words. This sacred object, refusing to be destroyed, had chosen its path, guided by the unseen hands of Providence. Robin said, "Thank God, I found it. Because if someone else had found it, they might not have known what it was, and its significance might have been lost, its sanctity disregarded.

"Fort Ross is a holy land," Robin continued, her voice lifting with fervor. "St. Innocent walked there. St. Peter left those shores before his martyrdom. St. Sebastian, St. Tikhon, and St. John of Shanghai and San Francisco all walked there. Five saints have blessed that ground with their presence."

She paused, letting the magnitude of these revelations sink in. "People need to know this story. They need to feel the spirit of Fort Ross, to understand the legacy of these saints and the sacredness of this place."

As Robin finished, the group sat in silence, the air thick with reverence and wonder. The story of the artist and the unburned icon of St. Peter the Aleut was more than a tale; it was a testament to faith, tradition, and the inexplicable mysteries that bind the past with the present.

Despite her growing connection to Orthodox Christianity, Robin did not convert immediately. It wasn't until 2021, during a pilgrimage to Anga in Siberia, the birthplace of St. Innocent, that everything fell into place. Invited by the Ministry of Culture and her longtime friends from an international historical society known as the Fort Ross Club, Robin embarked on a journey that would change her life.

In Anga, she and her companions—a group of priests, matushkas (priests' wives), and a nun—experienced a series of spiritually significant moments. They shared a feast with Metropolitan Maximilian, the ruling hierarch of the Siberian diocese. After learning more about St. Innocent at Fort Ross, and after her friend told him the story of the St. Peter the Aleut icon being found on the beach, the metropolitan asked Robin why she wasn't Orthodox. It was the first time anyone had asked her this question in the thirty years that she had been working at Fort Ross. The table, which included her dear priest friends, became quiet. They had wanted to ask her this question for a long time, and now they waited for her answer. Her response was heartfelt and sincere: she feared she wouldn't be a good Orthodox woman, daunted by the perceived rules and expectations. She had seen the rituals and liturgical traditions of the Orthodox Church with all the formal vestments, robes, bowing, and making the sign of the cross, and didn't understand it all.

The metropolitan's gentle reassurance, along with the support of the priests she had known for years, led Robin to a decision.

On September 8, 2021, on St. Innocent's birthday, in a river in Anga where he had been baptized, Robin was baptized into the Orthodox faith. The new name of Innokentia was given to her by the metropolitan in honor of St. Innocent Enlightener of North America, her new patron saint. Her first communion took place in the very church where St. Innocent had served as a young boy. She had always had a powerful connection to St. Innocent, not only because he visited Fort Ross but because he spoke to the depths of her heart with his warmth, humility, and love for children and Native people, which she also shared. Her baptism and communion across the world in the footsteps of St. Innocent himself was overwhelming. It's as if the love that Innokentia had held for St. Innocent for decades reverberated back to her in that river and church of Anga where St. Innocent had been received into Orthodoxy a century earlier.

Now, as an Orthodox Christian, Innokentia's journey had come full circle, her faith solidified in the very waters that had once baptized a saint she revered for decades. The Orthodox community that had embraced her for years now welcomed her fully as a sister in the faith, with parishioners and clergy alike celebrating her reception into the church.

Reflecting on her life, Innokentia felt gratitude for the path that had led her here. From her early days in Sacramento to her decades at Fort Ross, every step had been guided by a divine hand. Her story was one of patience, providence, and an unwavering faith that had always been a part of her. She didn't just find the icon of St. Peter on the beach of Fort Ross. St. Peter and St. Innocent found her.

Fort Ross, with its rich history and sacred legacy, remained a place of spiritual significance. Innokentia's work there, her connection to the saints, and her eventual conversion to Orthodox Christianity were all part of a larger tapestry that connected the past to the present. The fort, once a symbol of Russian presence in America, now also stood as a testament to the enduring power of faith and the spiritual journey of one woman.

As Innokentia looked to the future, she felt a renewed sense of purpose. She continued to share the stories of Fort Ross, St. Peter the Aleut, and St. Innocent, ensuring that their legacies lived on. Her mission was clear: to honor the saints, educate others about Orthodoxy, and celebrate the divine connections that had always guided her path.

Robin's discovery of St. Peter's icon on the sands of Fort Ross was more than a coincidence; it was a sign of the enduring presence of the saints in our lives, a reminder that their legacy transcends time and space, connecting us to the divine in ways we often least expect. As we honor the memory of St. Peter the Aleut, we are reminded of the power of faith to transform lives and illuminate the path to the divine.

A service at the chapel at Fort Ross

The Ancient Faith in the Modern World

SAINTS AMONG US

Gather my saints together unto me; those that have made a covenant with me by sacrifice.

(PSALM 50:5)

As the first light of dawn stretched across the Pacific, a golden hue bathed the misty coastline of California, revealing the weathered silhouette of Fort Ross. This sacred place, where land meets sea, has borne witness to centuries of history, a beacon of Orthodox faith and a testament to the enduring spiritual legacy on North America's western shores. Established in 1812 by the Russian-American Company, Fort Ross was more than just a trading post—it was a sanctuary, a haven graced by the presence of saints whose lives left an indelible mark on its history.

Nestled in a small bay called Bodega, fifty miles north of San Francisco, Fort Ross became a crucial outpost, a place where Russian settlers, Native Alaskan converts, and local Native Americans came together in a delicate balance of trade, faith, and cultural exchange. A modest chapel stood within the fort's wooden walls, its simple structure a contrast to the stark beauty of its surroundings. Here, the faithful gathered to sing and pray, their voices rising in unison, carried by the wind to the open sea.

Dedicated to the Holy Trinity, this chapel was the first Russian Orthodox chapel in North America outside of Alaska. Though it had no resident priest in its early years, the chapel served as the spiritual heart of the community. Over time, priest-missionaries visited from Sitka, bringing with them the sacraments and the Divine Liturgy, their presence breathing life into the wooden walls of the chapel. Among these visiting priests was Fr. Ioann Veniaminov, who would later be glorified as St. Innocent.

It was in 1836 that St. Innocent set foot on the grounds of Fort Ross. At that time, he was a Russian Orthodox priest, already renowned for his missionary work in Alaska. His visit to Fort Ross was part of a broader pastoral tour from Sitka, and during the five weeks he spent at the settlement, he left an indelible mark on the hearts of those who encountered him.

Saint Innocent celebrated the Divine Liturgy (the first in North America outside Alaska), administered the sacraments, and offered religious instruction to the colonists. He marveled at the harmonious coexistence of Russians, Native Alaskans, and local Native Californians—all three groups united in their

dedication to the Orthodox faith. His observations and interactions at Fort Ross would later enrich his missionary efforts.
His many years of service, his steadfast love of Alaska, and his
devout nature led to his elevation as Bishop of Alaska and eventually Metropolitan of Moscow. In 1977, his tireless work and
unwavering faith earned him the honor of sainthood.

Another figure who walked the sacred grounds of Fort Ross
was Jovan Dabovich, known as St. Sebastian upon his glorification. Born in San Francisco in 1863 to Serbian immigrant par-
ents, Sebastian's path to priesthood was marked by a devotion
to the Orthodox Church. Baptized aboard a Russian naval ship
off the Northern California coast, Sebastian's spiritual journey
was interwoven with the land of his birth.

In 1897, as a newly ordained priest, Fr. Sebastian visited
Fort Ross with Bishop Nicholas Ziorov. The visit stirred something within him. He was moved by the dilapidated state of the
chapel and cemetery, but instead of despair, he found hope and
purpose. Sebastian performed a religious rite over the graves,
recording his reflections in the Fort Ross Hotel Register. His
commitment to preserving the history of Orthodoxy in California was unwavering, a commitment that would lead to the
return of his relics to California in 2007. In 2015, his life of
service and dedication was recognized with sainthood.

St. Tikhon, known in the world as Basil Belavin, visited Fort
Ross in 1905, bringing with him the weight of leadership as the
head of the Orthodox Church in North America. St. Tikhon's
visit was a moment of reflection, a time to renew the spiritual
legacy of Fort Ross. Accompanied by Fr. Theodore Pashkovsky,
he found the chapel restored and once again a place of worship.

His tenure as head of the Orthodox Church in America was fraught with challenges—the rise of communism in Russia and the ensuing persecution of the Church—but through it all, St. Tikhon's dedication never wavered. His steadfastness was recognized when he was glorified in 1989.

One of the most beloved figures in Orthodox Christian history, St. John Maximovitch, also graced Fort Ross with his presence in 1963. Known as St. John the Wonderworker, he served as the Archbishop of San Francisco and Western America from 1962 until his death in 1966. During this visit, he served a Divine Liturgy at the historic site, which had been an important part of the Russian Orthodox Church's presence in North America. This event was significant as it marked a reconnection with the early Orthodox mission in America and the legacy of the first Orthodox Christians in California. St. John's visit to Fort Ross was one of the many acts that demonstrated his commitment to preserving and honoring the history of Orthodoxy in America. St. John's reputation for miracles and his compassion for his flock earned him a special place in the hearts of Orthodox Christians. His relics, housed in San Francisco, continue to draw pilgrims from around the world, each seeking his intercession and blessings.

Fort Ross, with its history of resilience and faith, remains a symbol of the Russian Orthodox presence on the West Coast of North America. The chapel, though rebuilt and restored multiple times, continues to be a place of worship, where the faithful gather to celebrate the Divine Liturgy, honor the saints who walked its grounds, and draw inspiration from their lives.

Fort Ross in 1960

Windows to Heaven

ORTHODOX ICONOGRAPHY AND ART

Moreover you shall make the tabernacle with ten curtains of fine woven linen and blue, purple, and scarlet thread; with artistic designs of cherubim you shall weave them.

(EXODUS 26:1)

Robin Innokentia's life was forever altered on the day she discovered the icon of Saint Peter the Aleut, which had washed back onto the beach at Fort Ross. The sacred artifact, uncovered in such an unexpected place, was more than a relic of the past—it was a tangible link to the rich spiritual heritage of the Orthodox Church in America. St. Peter the Aleut, a native Alaskan martyred for his faith, symbolized the spread of Orthodoxy to the New World and the deep roots it has established on this continent.

Orthodox iconography is more than art; it is a sacred practice, rooted in prayer, theology, and tradition. Iconographers, often living monastic lives or involved in the liturgical life of the Church, approach their work with reverence and spiritual discipline. The process of creating an icon involves prayer, fasting, and an intimate understanding of the saints and holy events depicted. This ensures that each icon is not only beautiful but also a theologically sound and spiritually uplifting representation of the divine.

The Second Commandment, which forbids the making of graven images, often raises questions about the use of icons in Orthodox Christianity. However, the incarnation of Christ—God made man—transformed our understanding of divine imagery. Icons are not mere decorations; they are windows to heaven, offering glimpses into the divine reality and bridging the earthly and heavenly realms. They are theological statements, conveying the truths of the faith in a visual form.

The history of iconography is marked by the iconoclast controversy of the eighth and ninth centuries, a period of intense debate and conflict over the use of religious images. Iconoclasts, influenced by Islamic prohibitions against images, sought to destroy icons, viewing them as idolatrous. In contrast, the iconodules, defenders of icons, argued that rejecting icons was akin to denying the incarnation of Christ. The Seventh Ecumenical Council in 787 affirmed the veneration of icons, and established the celebration of the Triumph of Orthodoxy in 843 restored their rightful place in worship.

Orthodox Christian iconography represents the fullness of the sacred images found in Solomon's Temple and early Jewish synagogues like the one at Dura-Europos. These earlier traditions used images to symbolize God's presence and to convey the stories and teachings of the faith. Orthodox iconography takes this tradition further not only by depicting biblical scenes and saints but also by serving as windows to the divine, offering the faithful a way to encounter and connect with the spiritual world.

The images in Solomon's Temple and the synagogue at Dura-Europos were rooted in the physical and historical aspects of the Jewish faith, but Orthodox icons transcend the physical to reveal spiritual truths. In the Orthodox Church, icons are more than just religious art—they are considered holy, created with prayer and reverence, and venerated as conduits of divine grace. Through icons, Orthodox Christians believe they can enter into a mystical communion with the figures depicted, whether they be Christ, the Theotokos (Mother of God), or the saints. Thus, Orthodox iconography completes and perfects the ancient tradition by fully embodying the theological and spiritual realities that the earlier images hinted at, making the invisible God visible and accessible to the faithful.

I still remember the first time I stepped into St. Dimitrius Greek Orthodox Church in Concord, California. The scent of incense was thick in the air, mingling with the quiet rustle of prayer books and the faint echo of chanting. My curiosity about Orthodoxy had led me here, but nothing could have prepared me for the overwhelming beauty that awaited me inside. The large image of Christ the Pantocrator in the dome seemed to gaze directly into my soul, His serene yet commanding presence leaving me speechless. In that moment, I felt an inexplicable connection to the divine, and I hung my head and wept.

My journey into Orthodox iconography continued with a visit to Holy Virgin Cathedral on Geary Street in San Francisco. This magnificent cathedral, one of the most beautiful places in America, houses the relics of St. John the Wonderworker. The moment I stepped inside, I was enveloped by a sense of peace and reverence. The intricate frescoes and gilded icons transported me to a heavenly realm, a place where the divine felt near and tangible. It was here, at the Holy Virgin Mary Bookstore on the corner, that I purchased my first icons, including an icon of the Image Not Made by Hands.

The story of the Image Not Made by Hands is one of the most fascinating in Christian tradition. According to holy tradition, a Syrian king named Abgar ruled the city-state of Edessa and suffered from a severe skin disease. Hearing of Jesus' miraculous healings, Abgar sent an envoy to invite Him to Edessa. Unable to go, Jesus instead pressed a cloth to His face, leaving a miraculous imprint of His features. This cloth, bearing the holy image, was sent to Abgar, who was healed upon receiving it. This first icon connects us directly with the body of the Savior and signifies the incarnation of God.

Equally compelling is the tradition of the first icon of the Virgin Mary, said to be painted by the Apostle Luke. This icon, known as the Hodegetria, or "She Who Shows the Way," depicts the Virgin Mary holding the Christ Child and pointing to Him as the source of salvation. It is a powerful visual testimony to the role of the Theotokos in leading the faithful to Christ. This icon has performed countless miracles, such as the rescue of Constantinople from the Arabs in the year 717. Though the original icon was destroyed during the Fall of

Constantinople in 1453, its reproductions continue to inspire devotion and reverence among the Orthodox faithful.

One of my most memorable visits was to St. Seraphim of Sarov Orthodox Church in Santa Rosa, California. There, I witnessed the breathtaking dome iconography recently completed by Fr. Patrick Doolan, a renowned iconographer trained by Leonid Ouspensky, one of the most famous Russian icon painters in the world. The true fresco technique, applied by Fr. Patrick and his assistant Fr. Moses, imbues the icons with a vividness and depth that is almost otherworldly. The dome, crowned with an image of Christ the Pantocrator, serves as a constant reminder of His omnipresence and love.

I've also visited St. Sava in Jackson and St. Andrew Antiochian Orthodox Church in Riverside, California. Each of these churches presents unique interpretations of Orthodox iconography, reflecting the diverse traditions within the faith. At St. Sava, the intricate Serbian-style frescoes convey a sense of history and continuity. Meanwhile, the icons at St. Andrew's, with their rich colors and expressive faces, drew me into the stories of the saints and the life of Christ.

In Los Angeles, the Holy Transfiguration Cathedral and St. Sophia Greek Orthodox Cathedral offered further insights into the vibrant world of Orthodox art. At Holy Transfiguration, the icons are both majestic and intimate, capturing the mysteries of the faith. St. Sophia, with its grand mosaics and detailed iconography, stands as a testament to the enduring legacy of Byzantine art. The harmony of light, color, and sacred imagery in these spaces speaks volumes about the depth and beauty of Orthodox worship.

Orthodox iconography continues to thrive in America, adapting to new contexts while preserving its ancient traditions. Iconographers like Heather Mackean exemplify this living tradition. Mackean, who has been painting in my hometown Santa Maria's Orthodox Church of the Annunciation for over twelve years, views her work as a vocation. Her commitment to the visual language of iconography and her dedication to capturing theological truths in her art are truly inspiring.

Heather Mackean's journey as an iconographer has taken her across the United States, from the East Coast to the West Coast. Her work in Santa Maria's Orthodox Church of the Annunciation is a testament to her skill and devotion. One of her notable pieces, a painting of Christ in gold and blue, graces the church's prominent gold dome. The interplay of light and color in her icons draws worshippers into a contemplative space, inviting them to encounter the divine.

Orthodox icons are far more than religious art; they are sacred tools that draw believers closer to God. My journey through various Orthodox churches and cathedrals, from the intimate setting of St. Dimitrius to the majestic Holy Virgin Cathedral, has increased my appreciation for this unique tradition. The icons, with their rich colors and symbolism, serve as constant reminders of the divine presence in our lives. They are indeed windows to heaven, opening our eyes to the beauty and mystery of the ancient faith in the modern world.

Each icon I encountered, each story I learned, and each church I visited contributed to a richer, more vibrant understanding of my faith. The journey of discovering Orthodox icons is never-ending, as each new encounter offers fresh insights and mystical connections to the divine.

Procession outside Holy Virgin Cathedral, San Francisco

St. Andrew Orthodox Church in Riverside, California

Re-enchanting America

AN ORTHODOX CHRISTIAN PERSPECTIVE ON BEAUTY AND SACREDNESS

*Wherefore seeing we also are compassed about with so great
a cloud of witnesses, let us lay aside every weight, and the sin
which doth so easily beset us, and let us run with patience the
race that is set before us.*

(HEBREWS 12:1)

In the heart of modern America, where the hum of machinery and the relentless flicker of screens dominate daily life, the sacred often feels distant. Yet, within this vast land lies the potential for spiritual renewal—a re-enchantment rooted in the ancient traditions of Orthodox Christianity. This vision invites us to rediscover the sacramental life, to see the world as a place brimming with divine presence, where every element of creation becomes a vessel of God's grace.

Orthodox Christianity views the world through the lens of sacramentality, where the mundane is imbued with mystery, transforming ordinary actions into holy acts. Baptism, the first of the sacraments, is not merely a ritual but a rebirth, an initiation into a life where every breath and every step is sanctified. Imagine the waters of baptism as a portal to a new creation, washing away the old and welcoming the new—a symbolic flood that echoes the cleansing of Noah's time and the liberation of the Israelites through the Red Sea.

This sacred perspective is at the core of the Orthodox understanding of the world. It is a worldview that challenges the secularization of modern life, where the divine is often relegated to the margins. Instead, Orthodoxy calls for a re-enchantment, a revival of the sacred in all aspects of life. This re-enchantment is not about retreating from the world but about engaging with it in a way that reveals the presence of God in every corner of creation.

In the Orthodox Christian tradition, the concepts of sacred space and sacred time are central to the experience of faith, providing a profound connection between the ancient and the modern, the temporal and the eternal. These elements serve as bridges that transport the faithful from the mundane realities of the world into the divine mysteries of God's Kingdom.

Orthodox sacred spaces—churches, monasteries, and even small chapels—are more than just physical structures; they are sanctified places where heaven and earth meet. These spaces are designed and consecrated to reflect the Kingdom of God, providing the faithful with a foretaste of the heavenly reality. The architecture of Orthodox churches, often rich in symbolism, guides the worshiper's senses toward the divine. The domes, icons, and incense, along with the layout of the sanctuary, create an environment where the sacred is palpably present.

The iconostasis, which separates the altar from the nave, symbolizes the boundary between the heavenly and earthly realms. Yet, this boundary is not a division but a veil that is drawn aside during the Divine Liturgy, allowing the worshiper to participate in the mysteries of faith. The church, therefore, becomes a space where the faithful are not just reminded of God's presence but are immersed in it, encountering the divine in a tangible, experiential way.

Time in Orthodox theology is understood in two distinct ways: *chronos* and *kairos*. Chronos refers to linear, chronological time—the time that governs daily life and historical progression. It is the time of the world, measurable and finite. In contrast, kairos is sacred time, a moment when the eternal breaks into the temporal, allowing the faithful to experience a reality that transcends the ordinary. Kairos is the time of God's intervention, the "appointed time" in which divine grace is encountered.

The Divine Liturgy is a manifestation of kairos. During the Liturgy, the congregation enters into a sacred time that is outside the constraints of chronos. Here, past, present, and future are united in the worship of God. The Liturgy is not a mere remembrance of past events, such as the Last Supper or the Resurrection, but a real participation in those events. Time becomes fluid, as the faithful are drawn into the eternal "now" of God's Kingdom.

In today's world, dominated by the relentless march of chronos, where time is often perceived as a commodity to be managed, the Orthodox understanding of sacred time and space stands in stark contrast. The modern world is consumed by the pressures of deadlines, schedules, and the pursuit of progress, often at the expense of spiritual depth. Sacred time and space offer a refuge from this ceaseless activity, inviting the faithful to step out of the hurried pace of modern life and into the timeless reality of God's presence.

The ancient faith of the Orthodox Church, with its emphasis on the sanctification of time and space, calls the modern believer to rediscover the sacred amidst the secular. In the sacred space of the church and the sacred time of the Liturgy, the faithful are reminded that life is not confined to the material and temporal but is rooted in the eternal and divine. This encounter with the sacred provides a counterbalance to the often fragmented and disorienting experience of modern life, offering a vision of reality that is whole, holy, and filled with grace.

Orthodoxy teaches that the world is not inherently secular; rather, it is called to be sanctified. This sanctification extends beyond people to places and practices. Consider the rural landscapes of America—the vast forests, the rolling plains, the mighty rivers. In these spaces, the faithful build churches, humble yet elegant, where the Divine Liturgy transforms ordinary bread and wine into the Body and Blood of Christ. These holy places become centers of spiritual life, oases of sanctity in a desert of secularism.

Orthodox Christians also bless their homes, workplaces, and even vehicles, invoking God's protection and presence in all aspects of life. Imagine a simple farmer's field, blessed at the start of the planting season, becoming a testament to the cooperation between human toil and divine grace.

As dawn gently breaks over the Pacific, casting a golden hue upon the misty coastline of California, it illuminates a world where the sacred transcends the ordinary. Fyodor Dostoevsky's declaration, "Beauty will save the world," resonates within the Orthodox Christian tradition. This beauty, manifested in the visual splendor and spiritual symbolism of Orthodox churches, cathedrals, and monasteries, reveals the transcendent truth that points to the divine.

Beauty in Orthodoxy is not merely aesthetic; it is a means of encountering God. The beauty of the liturgy, the icons, the architecture—all these are not just pleasing to the eye but are gateways to the divine. They engage the senses, drawing the faithful into a fuller experience of worship and communion with God.

Imagine stepping into an Orthodox church for the first time. The scent of incense fills the air, and the soft glow of candlelight dances across the icons. The chanting of the choir reverberates through the nave, a melody that seems to bridge the gap between heaven and earth. Every element of the church is designed to draw the worshiper into a sacred space where the presence of God is palpable.

Orthodox sacred spaces are intentionally designed to evoke this sense of beauty. The domes of the church, often adorned with icons of Christ Pantocrator, remind the faithful that Christ is the ruler of all, reigning from heaven. The iconostasis, with its intricate icons, serves as a visual representation of the communion of saints, those who have gone before us and who now stand before the throne of God.

The icons themselves are not merely religious art; they are windows to heaven, offering a glimpse into the divine mysteries. The faces of the saints, serene and filled with the light of Christ, invite the faithful to contemplate the life of holiness to which they are called. The colors, the forms, the gestures—all are imbued with theological meaning, pointing beyond themselves to the reality of God.

Pilgrimage is another powerful expression of the re-enchantment of the world. In Orthodox Christianity, pilgrimage is not just a physical journey but a spiritual one, a journey toward God. Pilgrims travel to holy sites, seeking to encounter the divine in a more personal way. These holy places, whether ancient monasteries or modern cathedrals, are sanctuaries where the veil between heaven and earth is thin.

Picture a pilgrim journeying to a remote monastery in the Appalachian Mountains. The serene landscape, a stark contrast to the noise and chaos of daily life, invites the pilgrim into communion with God. The monastic bells call them to prayer, the ancient chants envelop them in a timeless liturgy, and the sacred icons draw them into communion with the divine. These holy places are sanctuaries of peace, offering a foretaste of the Kingdom of God.

My own journey into the heart of Orthodox beauty began in San Francisco, where the sacred and the urban blend seamlessly. Approaching Holy Virgin Cathedral, its Russian-style onion domes and intricate iconography transported me to the spiritual heart of Orthodoxy. Stepping inside, I was immediately struck by the atmosphere of reverence and awe. The entrance led me into the narthex, the outermost section of the church. This area serves as a transition space, where the faithful pause and prepare themselves before entering the more sacred parts of the church. In the narthex, I saw people lighting candles—a simple yet reflective act symbolizing prayers offered to God, the light of Christ illuminating the darkness, and the saints who intercede for us.

Passing through the narthex is like stepping through a time portal to the ancient world. The nave, the main body of the church where the congregation gathers, is adorned with beautiful icons depicting Christ, the Virgin Mary, and the saints. These icons are not merely decorative; they are considered windows to heaven, inviting the faithful into a contemplation of the divine. The rich colors and serene expressions of the holy figures depicted in the icons filled me with a sense of peace and connection to the history and community of the Church.

At the far end of the nave stands the iconostasis, a wall of icons and doors that separates the nave from the altar, or sanctuary. The iconostasis itself is a powerful symbol of the boundary between the heavenly and earthly realms, with the icons serving as intermediaries. The altar area, where the most sacred parts of the liturgy take place, is reserved for the clergy and is considered the holiest part of the church. The beauty and order of the sanctuary reminded me that worship in the Orthodox Church is participation in the heavenly liturgy.

One of the most striking aspects of the Orthodox liturgy is the ornate clerical garments, harkening back to the vestments worn by priests in the ancient Temple of Jerusalem. Each piece of the vestments worn by the clergy holds symbolic meaning. Seeing the clergy vested in these garments, I realized that every aspect of the liturgy is imbued with layers of meaning, each gesture and item pointing to higher spiritual truths. The vestments transform the ordinary into the extraordinary, setting the clergy apart for their sacred duties and visually conveying the glory and majesty of the heavenly kingdom.

The chanting in an Orthodox service is another element that moved me. The hymns and prayers are often sung in a chant that echoes the ancient traditions of the Church. The melodic and rhythmic chanting creates an atmosphere that elevates the soul, drawing the congregation into a communal act of worship. The words of the hymns are rich with theological significance, often recounting the lives of the saints, the events of Christ's life, and the mysteries of the faith.

The mission of the Church extends beyond the baptism of individuals to the baptism of cultures, places, and practices. This holistic approach seeks to transform society from within, infusing it with the values and truths of the Orthodox faith. The arts, sciences, and social structures are all seen as arenas for this transformative work. Imagine artists inspired by the beauty of the Divine Liturgy, their works reflecting the transcendent glory of God. Scientists approach their research with a sense of wonder, seeing in the intricacies of creation the hand of the Creator. Social activists, guided by the teachings of Christ, work to alleviate suffering and promote justice, their efforts rooted in a vision of the sanctity of every human life.

Orthodox Christianity views all of creation as sacred, a testament to the Creator's love and wisdom. This perspective stands in stark contrast to the sterility and utilitarianism of modern technological society. The natural world, with its rhythms and cycles, is a continuous revelation of God's glory. In a world dominated by mechanization, the Orthodox vision calls for a return to a more harmonious relationship with nature. The stewardship of the earth is seen not as a mere duty but as a sacred responsibility. The fields, forests, and rivers are not just resources to be exploited but gifts to be cherished and preserved.

Re-enchanting America with an Orthodox Christian perspective is a call to see the world anew, to recognize the divine presence in every aspect of life. It is a call to live sacramentally, to sanctify our surroundings, to pray without ceasing, and to draw inspiration from the saints and holy places. Amid the busyness and distractions of modern life, this vision offers a path to meaning and fulfillment. It invites us to slow down, to seek the sacred in the ordinary, and to embrace a life filled with wonder and grace. As we embark on this journey of re-enchantment, we are reminded that the Kingdom of God is not a distant reality but a present and living truth, waiting to be discovered in every moment and every place.

Epilogue

THE LIVING FAITH OF ORTHODOXY IN AMERICA

Finally, brothers and sisters, whatever is true, whatever is noble, whatever is right, whatever is pure, whatever is lovely, whatever is admirable—if anything is excellent or praiseworthy—think about such things.

(PHILIPPIANS 4:8)

America stands at a crossroads, where history meets the present, and the timeless beauty of the Orthodox Christian faith continues to illuminate lives. This ancient faith, rich in tradition, transcends ethnic boundaries and invites all to experience the Divine Life handed down by Christ through His apostles.

The lives of saints like St. Peter the Aleut, St. Innocent, St. Sebastian Dabovich, St. Tikhon, and St. John the Wonderworker showcase the powerful impact of Orthodoxy in

America. St. Peter the Aleut's martyrdom sowed the seeds of the Gospel in American soil. St. Innocent's educational and linguistic contributions laid a foundation for Orthodoxy's growth. St. Sebastian Dabovich's pioneering spirit as the first American-born Orthodox priest highlights the faith's adaptability. St. Tikhon's unifying efforts and St. John the Wonderworker's miracles in San Francisco further underscore Orthodoxy's enduring power.

Orthodox Christianity's visual splendor is a testament to its theological depth. Icons, as "windows to heaven," and stunning church architecture, from the majestic domes of St. Sophia Cathedral in Los Angeles to the serene beauty of St. Herman of Alaska Monastery in Platina, inspire awe and elevate the soul.

Orthodoxy in America is universal, embracing all who seek the truth. It's a living expression of the Divine Life, a continuous tradition faithfully preserved. The faith offers a holistic spirituality, emphasizing sacraments like the Eucharist and the prayers of the Divine Liturgy, a foretaste of the heavenly banquet. Monasteries like Holy Assumption in Calistoga, California and St. Anthony's in Florence, Arizona provide spiritual havens for prayer and contemplation.

In addition to writing more books and developing film projects, I hope to travel and visit Orthodox communities around the world. Each pilgrimage enriches my understanding of the universal nature of the Church and the diverse ways in which the Orthodox faith is lived out in different cultures. Whether I am in a bustling city or a remote monastery, I feel a sense of unity with my fellow Orthodox Christians, united by our shared faith and love for Christ.

Looking back on my journey, I am filled with gratitude for the many blessings and experiences that have shaped my faith. The path to Orthodoxy was not always easy, but it was guided by the grace of God and the intercessions of the saints. My encounters with remarkable individuals like Robin and James, my pilgrimages to holy sites, and my service to the Church have all been part of a greater plan, leading me closer to the fullness of the Orthodox faith.

I invite you to explore Orthodoxy. Visit an Orthodox church or monastery, attend a Divine Liturgy, and learn about the saints. Orthodoxy offers a rich understanding of the Christian faith, rooted in ancient traditions, inviting believers to encounter the living God.

The Orthodox Church is a vibrant community striving to embody Christ's teachings. It is a place where the ancient faith meets the modern world, offering a timeless message of hope and salvation.

As you close these pages, remember, this could be the beginning of a new chapter in your spiritual journey. May the stories of the saints, the beauty of the art and architecture, and the depth of the Orthodox faith inspire you to seek fullness of life in Christ and share the light of Orthodoxy with the world.

In the words of St. Seraphim of Sarov, "Acquire the Spirit of Peace, and thousands around you will be saved." May the peace and joy of the Orthodox faith guide you on your journey. The ancient faith of the Orthodox Church is a light in the darkness, a beacon of hope, and a living expression of the Divine Life, ready to transform lives and renew the world.

Come and see.

Timeline of Orthodoxy in America

SELECTED HIGHLIGHTS

The narrative of Orthodox Christianity in America is a rich tapestry woven with the threads of diverse immigrant experiences, including Russian, Greek, Syrian, Serbian, and Romanian communities, among others. Their collective contributions have profoundly shaped the Orthodox faith in America, especially in California.

1794: The Seeds of Orthodoxy in Alaska

Amid the majestic Alaskan wilderness, the stage was set for an enduring legacy. On September 24, 1794, St. Herman and the monks of Valaam, sent by Empress Catherine the Great with the Russian-American Company, arrived in Kodiak, Alaska. These pioneers planted the seeds of Orthodox Christianity in North America, creating a spiritual foundation that would grow and flourish over centuries. The echoes of their prayers still resonate in the winds that sweep across the Alaskan tundra, a testimony to their unwavering faith and dedication.

1812: The Founding of Fort Ross

In 1812, the Russian-American Company established Fort Ross on the rocky northern coast of California. This fortified outpost, perched high above the tumultuous waves of the Pacific, became the first beacon of Orthodox Christianity in California. The settlers, resilient and faithful, laid the foundations for what would become a significant spiritual legacy. The sound of the ocean crashing against the cliffs below seemed to carry the hymns sung within the modest chapel, a melody that would echo through generations.

1815: The Martyrdom of Saint Peter the Aleut

Fast forward to 1815, near the serene yet perilous coastline of Southern California. Peter the Aleut, an Alaskan native from Kodiak, found himself ensnared by Spanish soldiers. His unwavering refusal to renounce his Orthodox faith in favor of Catholicism led to his brutal martyrdom. Peter's steadfast declaration, "I am a Christian; I will not betray my faith," echoes through the ages. Glorified as a martyr, his legacy is uniquely connected with the faith's growth in California. His sacrifice, made on these shores so distant from his homeland, became a cornerstone of the spiritual edifice being built in America.

1824: The First Diocese

The Holy Synod of Russia established the Diocese of Alaska in 1824, the first Orthodox diocese in North America, solidifying the church's presence and influence in the New World. The establishment of the diocese was like the planting of a great tree, its roots digging deep into the American soil, destined to grow tall and strong, providing shelter for the faithful.

Mid-1820s: Fort Ross Chapel

By the mid-1820s, the colonists at Fort Ross had built a modest chapel, the Holy Trinity Chapel, the first Russian Orthodox structure in North America outside of Alaska. This humble edifice stood as a testament to their faith and resilience. Within its wooden walls, the faithful gathered, their prayers rising like incense, creating a spiritual anchor that would weather the storms of time.

1836: The Arrival of Saint Innocent

In 1836, a Russian schooner carrying the revered Fr. Ioann Veniaminov, later known as St. Innocent, landed at Fort Ross. This dedicated priest brought with him from Alaska a steadfast commitment to missionary work. Over the course of his visit, he baptized new converts, performed marriages, and celebrated the Divine Liturgy, leaving an indelible mark on the fledgling Orthodox community. His presence was like a breath of fresh air, invigorating the spiritual life of the settlement and setting in motion a wave of faith that would ripple across the continent.

1857: The First Orthodox Society in San Francisco

By 1857, the spiritual landscape of California began to transform with the founding of the first Orthodox Society in San Francisco. Ten years later, it was officially incorporated as the Greek Russian Slavonian Orthodox Eastern Church and Benevolent Society. During these early years, the Orthodox faithful were served by chaplains from Russian Navy ships that frequented San Francisco Bay. The society's establishment was like a lighthouse, guiding the Orthodox faithful in the growing city, its light shining across the waters of the bay.

1867: Alaska Becomes American

Alaska's transfer to the United States in 1867 marked a significant transition. The Russian Orthodox mission adapted to American jurisdiction, continuing its vital work among the Native and settler populations. This change was a new chapter in the story of Orthodoxy in America, one that would see the faith grow and adapt to the changing landscape of the New World.

1867: The Vision of Saint Innocent

Shortly after Alaska's transfer, St. Innocent, then Metropolitan of Moscow, saw this as a providential opportunity for Orthodoxy to penetrate deeper into American soil. He envisioned San Francisco as the new spiritual hub, proposing its climate and strategic location for the Orthodox vicariate. His vision included the use of English in liturgy and instruction, ensuring that Orthodoxy could reach and resonate with a broader audience. In 1868, San Francisco saw the establishment of its first Russian Orthodox parish, which would eventually be known as Holy Trinity Cathedral. This marked a significant shift, with San Francisco replacing Sitka as the diocesan seat. The church became a spiritual haven for the growing Orthodox community, laying the foundation for future growth.

1873: The Arrival of Saint Sebastian

In 1873, Hieromonk Sebastian Dabovich arrived in San Francisco, a city he would frequently return to in his missionary efforts. In 1893 his journey took him to Jackson, California, where he discovered a vibrant Serbian Orthodox community. His encouragement led to the construction of the St. Sava Orthodox Church, consecrated in 1894. Fr. Sebastian's relentless dedication to spreading the faith laid the groundwork for Orthodoxy's expansion throughout California. His missionary efforts were like seeds sown in fertile soil, destined to bear fruit for generations to come.

1890: Translating the Faith

In 1890, Bishop Vladimir (Sokolovsky) spearheaded efforts to translate liturgical texts into English, broadening the reach and accessibility of Orthodoxy to new converts and English-speaking communities. This was a key moment in making the faith more accessible, a bridge between the old world and the new.

1899: The Impact of Bishop Tikhon

In 1899, Bishop Tikhon visited the Serbian Orthodox community in Jackson, California, welcomed by Fr. Sebastian Dabovich. Bishop Tikhon's commitment to serving all Orthodox Christians equally, regardless of their ethnic backgrounds, was evident in his cross-country tour, which concluded in San Francisco. His tenure as the head of the Orthodox Church in America saw significant growth and the establishment of a solid foundation for future generations.

1900–1920: Russian, Greek, Syrian, Serbian, and Romanian Immigration

The early twentieth century witnessed waves of immigration from Russia, Greece, Syria, Serbia, and Romania. These communities brought their rich traditions and fervent faith, establishing ethnic parishes and enriching the tapestry of American Orthodoxy. Their contributions were vital in the expansion and diversification of the Orthodox Christian presence in California.

1905: St. Tikhon's Seminary

The first Orthodox seminary in America, St. Tikhon's Orthodox Theological Seminary, was founded in 1905 in South Canaan, Pennsylvania. This institution became a cornerstone for training clergy and nurturing the faith.

1906: *Fort Ross Becomes a Part of State Lands*

Fort Ross was donated to State Parks as one of the first ten state parks in California. In that same year, the 1906 earthquake collapsed the Fort Ross Chapel.

1907: *Self-Governance Begins*

The All-American Sobor (Council) in 1907 marked the beginning of self-governance for the American Orthodox Church, setting the stage for greater autonomy and growth.

1915: *Fort Ross Chapel Reconstructed*

No services were held for many years.

1917: *A Turning Point*

The Russian Revolution in 1917 disrupted support for the American Orthodox Church, pushing it toward greater independence and self-sufficiency. The upheaval in the old world necessitated a new approach in the new, fostering a resilience that would see the faith through challenging times.

1921: *Greek Orthodox Archdiocese*

The establishment of the Greek Orthodox Archdiocese of America in 1921 marked the official presence of Greek Orthodoxy, further diversifying and enriching American Orthodoxy.

1925–Present: *The Revival of Fort Ross*

Since 1925, the Holy Trinity Chapel at Fort Ross has been the site of annual Divine Liturgies, drawing Orthodox faithful from across the state. The chapel, rebuilt and restored multiple times, stands as a symbol of the enduring Orthodox presence in California. Each year, on Memorial Day and the Fourth of July, the faithful gather to celebrate the Divine Liturgy, honoring the legacy of those who brought Orthodoxy to these shores.

1933: Antiochian Orthodox Archdiocese

The Antiochian Orthodox Christian Archdiocese of North America was established in 1933, serving the growing number of Middle Eastern Orthodox Christians and adding to the vibrant mosaic of American Orthodoxy.

1962: The Legacy of Saint John the Wonderworker

In 1962 Archbishop John Maximovitch came to San Francisco, a man whose life was marked by spiritual depth and miracles. His tenure in San Francisco was challenging, marked by efforts to heal divisions within the community and oversee the construction of the new cathedral dedicated to the Joy of All Who Sorrow Icon of the Mother of God. His repose in 1966 and subsequent glorification in 1994 cemented his legacy as a beloved saint and a guiding light for the faithful.

1965–1980: Post-World War II Immigration

The period following World War II saw continued immigration from Orthodox Christian countries, further establishing the faith's presence in California. New parishes were founded, and the cultural contributions of Greek, Syrian, Serbian, and Romanian communities enriched the spiritual landscape.

1970: Autocephaly for the OCA

In 1970, the Orthodox Church in America (OCA) received autocephaly from the Russian Orthodox Church, becoming fully independent and self-governing. This was a moment of maturation for the Church in America, a declaration of its readiness to stand on its own in the spiritual landscape of the New World.

1982: The Monastic Vision of Fr. Seraphim Rose

Born in 1934, Eugene Rose's journey to Orthodoxy led him to the wilderness of Northern California, where he cofounded the St. Herman of Alaska Monastery in Platina. Known as Fr. Seraphim, his writings and teachings drew many to the Orthodox faith. His death in 1982 and the subsequent veneration of his memory underscored the enduring impact of his spiritual journey.

1994: St. Herman Glorified

The glorification of St. Herman of Alaska by the Orthodox Church in America in 1994 celebrated his foundational role in American Orthodoxy, honoring his enduring legacy. His life and witness continue to inspire the faithful, a testament to the power of faith lived out in the stark beauty of Alaska.

2024: The Glorification of Saint Olga of Alaska

In a momentous event, 2024 witnessed the glorification of Saint Olga of Alaska, further enriching the spiritual heritage of Orthodox Christianity in America and honoring her significant contributions to the faith.

All Saints of North America Hymnography[1]

A hymn is sung during the evening Vespers service on the third Sunday of Pentecost to commemorate All Saints of North America. The feast day is a reminder that the Orthodox Church has been established in America and that the gates of hell will never prevail against it.

Come, let us praise the Saints of North America, holy and venerable monastics, and glorious men, women, and children, both known and unknown. Through their words and deeds in various walks of life, by the grace of the Spirit, they achieved great things. Now, as they stand in the presence of Christ to glorify Him, they pray for us to celebrate their memory. Come, let us assemble to honor the luminaries of North America—the holy bishops who confirmed our faith, the righteous dwellers in the wilderness, and those of the spiritual life.

---

1 From *Liturgical Hymns of the Orthodox Church in America.*

Let us cry out to them in joy: All Saints of North America, known and unknown, pray to God for us.

As the brightest sun and the brilliance of the stars, the precious feast of the Saints of North America calls us to set our hearts on their example and follow their path of faith. Come, let us assemble today and praise the elect of North America. Having fought valiantly, they persevered in the faith, receiving their crowns of victory from God. We ask them to deliver us from every calamity and sorrow as we keep their holy memory in faith and devotion.

The Earth rejoices, and the heavens are glad as we praise the Saints of North America for their spiritual fortitude and purity of heart. They drove away multitudes of demons and enlightened many people with the light of the Orthodox faith, confirming our land and prevailing over us with God's mercy and truth.

Rise up, mountains of Pennsylvania, and waters of the Great Lakes. Rejoice, the upper plains of Canada, for the elect of Christ who dwelt in you are glorified. Men and women who left their homes, armed with faith, hope, and patience, courageously fought the good fight. Comforted by the beauty of the Orthodox faith, they endured many hardships and sufferings, never failing to worship God in spirit and truth, and unyielding in their devotion to His most pure mother.

Come, assembly of the faithful, and with love let us praise

the holy women, men, and children—those known to us and those known only to God. Let us cry out to them: Rejoice, all Saints of North America, and pray to God for us.
Glory to the Father, and to the Son, and to the Holy Spirit. Rejoice, continents of North America, for God has illuminated you by the holy gospel. Rejoice, every province and town which raised citizens of the heavenly kingdom. Rejoice, venerable Father Herman, first Saint of our land. Rejoice, martyr Juvenaly, for your blood has watered the seed of faith in Alaska. Rejoice, holy bishops, and righteous priests Alexis and John. Rejoice, Saints of North America, for we implore you to pray to Christ our God for the salvation of our souls. Today, as we celebrate the memory of all the Saints of North America, let us praise them as is fitting. For the love of Christ, they became poor in material wealth but rich in spirit. Mourning, they were comforted; thirsting for righteousness, they were satisfied. Merciful, they obtained mercy; pure in heart, they beheld the image of God. As peacemakers, they became God's children. Persecuted and tortured for righteousness, they now rejoice in heaven and fervently pray to the Lord for His mercy on our souls.

Let us praise with one accord the protectress of our land, our Queen. Rejoice, for you have graced our land with your favor, pouring abundant grace upon it. The church in America joyously celebrates your precious protection and the multitude of your miracles. Do not deprive us now of your mercies, O Lady. Look with favor upon us in our adversities and afflictions and raise us up by your powerful intercession.

As a bountiful harvest of the sowing of salvation, the Saints of North America offer to the Lord all the saints who have shone in them. By their prayers, keep the church in our land in abiding peace through the mercy of the All-Merciful One.

About the Author

ROBERT JOHN HAMMOND is an accomplished screenwriter, author, and producer whose work has garnered awards and acclaim across various creative platforms. He holds a Master of Fine Arts (MFA) in Creative Writing and has shared his expertise as a professor of screenwriting and creative writing at Southern New Hampshire University and Brandman University, a division of Chapman. His academic career also includes guest lectures on film history at Mills College and the University of Maryland.

Hammond's diverse filmography includes contributions to the documentary *One Day on Earth* and the insightful exploration *Bohemian Grove*. He also adapted his novel *C. B. DeMille: The Man Who Invented Hollywood* into a biopic, capturing the life and legacy of one of cinema's pioneers.

As a bestselling author, Hammond's works span a range of topics, reflecting his versatility and depth. His notable titles include *Life After Debt* (Career Press), *Credit Secrets* (Paladin Press), *Identity Theft* (Career Press), *The Light* (New Way Press), and *Transformed by Writing: How to Change Your Life and Change Your World with the Power of Story* (New Way Press). Additionally, he served as editor and contributor to the anthology *Roads Less Traveled: Journeys to Orthodoxy* (Divine Ascent Press), further showcasing his commitment to exploring transformative narratives.

Made in the USA
Las Vegas, NV
19 December 2024